Praise for Letters to My Daughters

Very Inspiring

"I love this book because it shows a fathers love for his daughters in a positive light. With so many absentee fathers out there, it is nice to find a book that celebrates the strong bond of the father/daughter relationship, and *Letters to My Daughters* does just that in bringing about a warmth and truth that confirms that every young girl needs her father. I would highly recommend this book to not only fathers, mothers and daughters, but to the entire family; for it takes a village to raise a child. Thank you Avery Washington for presenting a great work for your daughters and our young girls who will one day grow into beautiful women, because someone took the time out to say I care."
~ La Trisha McIntosh - Beautifully Said Magazine

Superbly Written

"I found *Letters to My Daughters* to be a song, a testament of a father's love and advice, wisely written so that everyone can gain these drops of wisdom, wrapped in love."
~ Author, Gina Humber

Literary Blessing

"*Letters to My Daughters* deserves to be on coffee tables across the nation. This book has inspired me so much. Though, I do not have a daughter, I have a son, but somehow the jewels embedded in the passion and determination that Avery is presenting to his daughters I can still share and have shared with my son. Being an adult, I am still my father's daughter and in his physical absence from my life, this book echoes what my father has expressed for me during my life while he was alive. In such a dark world we are sometimes forced to live in, it is true inspiration and love for family where the light begins and I appreciate this book. I thank Avery for sharing his love for his daughters with those of us who have been blessed by this book! Ready for the next one."
~ Tony D.

Don't Let The Title Fool You!

"This gem of a book captures Avery Washington's sheer talent, humility and love for not only his daughters, but for wives, husbands and sons. This book has content for just about anyone who needs

family-focused letters to share or simply create a special love note to leave out for a surprise for their daughters or wife to read for any occasion.
Although my daughter is all grown up now and has a daughter of her own, this book has inspired me to love her even more. The bonus quotes in back of the book are unequivocally "must reads" for anyone striving to succeed with their daughters, entire family or in their business ventures." ~ Gilly

Love

"Excellent tool for developing a great relationship with your daughters. Great job Avery!" ~ Joseph

Powerful

"Mr. Washington, you have really painted pictures through the love you possess for your daughters and wife, but most of all, for God as a platform for single and married parents. I can witness and attest to this love, because my brother shared it with me. My dad was in the world, but God always have things according to His will!"
~ Diane Washington - Robinson

A Treasure Trove of Love in the First-Degree

"The fact that a man would unleash to his three daughters, a road map, with explicit directions leading to self-esteem, compassion and the purpose of God in their lives is rare at any age. What a treasure trove of love in the first-degree Mr. Washington has bequeathed to his three daughters by writing this book. A book that has sealed the purpose of his family tree; a work that will surely be passed down for generations to come. If you are a father or mother who has daughters, do yourself a favor and pay it forward by seeding this book to them. You won't regret it." ~ George Green

This Book Touches My Heart!

"Every time I read this book I cry, because I've been hurt so much in my life. It really touches my heart!" ~ Carla K.

Very Inspiring

"This book is one that every mother and father should get for their daughters! It shows a young girl that she should first love God and self before investing love in a man. This book shows how a real father loves his daughters!" ~ Krystal

Empowering!

"This book is very empowering to daughters of all ages' and should be read in all schools with open discussions to help in the healing and growth of many of our young women in the world today. Avery Washington brilliantly combines the love of God with self-love into inspirational stories while poetically engaging the readers into a world of love, triumph and understanding."
~ Malcolm Patterson - Against The Grain Magazine

Also by Avery Washington

Just Speaking My Mind
Letters to My Daughters 1st Edition
Mother

LEGACY

LEGACY

2ND EDITION OF PROFOUND BESTSELLER
LETTERS TO MY DAUGHTERS

By

AVERY WASHINGTON

Foreword by Hilton J. La Salle III, Ed. D.

Happie Publishing
Katy, TX

Happie Publishing
Katy, TX 77494
inspiration@happiepublishing.com
832-422-8977 or 832-800-8962

LEGACY: 2nd Edition of Profound Bestseller Letters to My
Daughters

ISBN - 13: 978-0-9990420-0-7
LCCN 2017908339

Dedication

I have been empowered and inspired to become a better man, husband, father and human being from all the beautiful strong women God has blessed me with in my life. This book is dedicated to all of you. Thank you.

A special dedication goes out to my three beautiful daughters Diamond, Breanna and Averianna Washington! "My undying love for you has allowed me to share my heart with the world and I will continue to encourage you three to pursue your dreams and turn them into your reality!"
I Love You!
Your Father and Daddy Always,
Avery Washington

Legacy - 1. A gift by will especially of money or other personal property.

2. Something transmitted by or received from an ancestor, predecessor or from the past.

My Legacy - Sharing my God given gift of love, empowerment, inspiration and encouragement through profound written affirmations of love to my daughters and everyone reading my words that will transcend these pages and forever be embedded in their hearts.

Contents

*Added Content

Foreword

Grammy award winners Stevie Wonder and Luther Vandross, in addition to many other famous musicians, have vocalized reflective songs embodying their passion of "a fathers love." In 1976, legendary Motown artist Stevie Wonder released a song titled "Isn't She Lovely," describing his deep affection for his newborn daughter. Mr. Wonder affectionately expressed that his (1) minute old daughter is wonderful, precious, and that she was created by love and heaven sent from God. In 2003, world renowned singer Luther Vandross released his hit song "Dance with My Father," recounting his childhood experiences dancing with his father, then being carried off to bed by his father, and how from his bedroom afar he'd secretly watch his mother and father dance all night. Mr. Vandross continued elegantly singing, "I knew for sure I was loved" and "if I could get another chance to dance with my father again." I am confident that these two songs touched the souls of millions of people as a father's love can have an everlasting effect on all parties involved. To put it differently, subconsciously, we all internalize deep developmental dilemmas of fatherhood either as a parent or as a child. Avery Washington shares with us his passion for being a father, as Stevie and Luther hit home to millions; *Legacy*: 2*nd Edition to Letters to My Daughters* does the same.

At a time when America's moral fabric is ripped, Avery reintroduces "a father's love" to the world as an essential value of self-restoration and healing for all. A core value in self-restoration is self-esteem, a person's sense of self-worth, which correlates to self-confidence.

For daughters, having an engaged father during her developmental years is significant and can be a natural nurturing experience for self-esteem as the need for self-image and self-concepts to be congruent. Avery's God invoking literature is designed to initiate, secure, and reinforce a father's love to and for his daughters.

Specifically, Avery's focus is on the father-daughter relationship from birth through young adulthood, however, the core of this relationship is eternal. The father's role is to be a strong leader above all and for many families he is perceived as the provider and protector. During the early developmental "subconscious" years, for a young girl, her father is symbolized as her savior, hero, and when she is with him this may be the safest place in the universe for her.

Let us take a closer look... When a middle-aged mother reflects on rearing her young son, most of her reflection of this parenting is indicative of her relationship with her father and grandfathers during her developmental years. This afterthought indirectly guides her rearing method for her young son in a subconscious manner - in autopilot mode. Without completely understanding her experience with her own father and grandfathers, she does what is comforting and familiar (may not always be the most effective approach) in the rearing process.

Another case is a young father gazing into the eyes of his newborn daughter and is now reflective of his new responsibility. At this moment, subconsciously, the new young father begins to think about the men in his life and their relationships with their spouses as a guide. There are countless scenarios of relationships all of which the "father-daughter relationship" is accountable for the manifestation of new effective an ineffective affairs.

I am truly blessed to have had discussions with my eighteen-year-old daughter about the context in which *Legacy* was written. The time we shared reminded me of the intelligent young woman she has become. "Haivyn, I am extremely proud of you and you have become the beautiful person God designed you to be. As you enter your first year of college and transition into young adulthood, you will always be my little angel. Daddy loves you!"

Hilton J. La Salle III, Ed. D.

Introduction

A few years ago my undying love for my three daughters inspired me to write a very profound book filled with poetic stories of encouragement, empowerment, inspiration and love affirmations with the aspirations to leave a legacy that they could learn from and be proud of. I emphasized the importance of embracing the love of God and self in this book, because I never wanted my daughters to desperately seek love from man. The title of the book was *Letters to My Daughters.* I shared my innermost feelings and thoughts in the book, because I wanted the book to be heartfelt while the words transcend the pages piercing the hearts of my daughters, so that they would forever feel my presence inside of their hearts. Little did I know that God was using me to reach a much larger audience.

Letters to My Daughters resonated rapidly with adult women and became a number one bestseller in multiple categories. Many women began to willingly share their stories of father and daughter relationships. Some expressed their desires to have a father in their lives during their upbringing to give them the love and guidance that they felt was needed.

Others shared stories of the great relationships with their fathers and how it had a positive impact on their lives.

Men also began to speak on the positive impact the book has had in their lives. During a radio interview one of the male guest expressed to me that I had no idea of how the book has helped him with his relationship with his daughter. After getting off the air, his wife instant messaged me on Facebook and expressed gratitude and shared with me that they were using some of the writings in *Letters to My Daughters* to help with the raising of their daughter. Wow! Can you imagine that? I just thought I was being a loving father to my daughters.

The birth of my latest book *Legacy* was created due to the overwhelming response I have received from readers. I strongly felt that I needed to release a second edition with more profound poetic stories and quotes, because many of our daughters are being misled in today's world by vulgar images and words broadcasted daily through television, movies, radio, music videos and other media outlets. We need to get back to teaching our young women that the love of God and self are two important forms of love needed to give them all the confidence, strength, wisdom, self-esteem and guidance that they will need to help them succeed. I now leave to all of you my *Legacy*!

I also will be introducing to you a poem written by my ten-year-old daughter Averianna Sydnie Washington. The title of her poem is *True Colors* and this is also the title of her upcoming book of poetry!

POEMS

Legacy

As your father, it's my responsibility
To leave with you a
Legacy
That will transcend these pages
And become embedded inside of your heart for
Eternity.

My legacy is not in the form of degrading false narratives
That America has been spreading for
Centuries;
It's a three-stranded cord composed poetically and filled
With expressions that are emotional, social and spiritual that
Gives you the tools to rise successfully.

Our faith in God has always provided us with
The strength and unity needed to uplift our
Communities.
No weaponry formed against our faith and moral beliefs
Will ever come between the love and loyalty we have for
Family.

I zealously share with you that we come from a lineage of
Kings and Queens of great
Integrity!
We are a proud people with great ambition and positivity
With the strength to overcome systemic racism and slavery,
Because we are royalty!

I readily and acceptably take on the responsibility of
Providing you with the love, security and stability
To empower you emotionally.
There is more to life than reading, writing and geometry.
Having a keen sense of self and being strong mentally
Will help you succeed socially.

God has blessedly bestowed upon me the special gift of you
And the creation of you is God's greatest
Masterpiece!
I love you and will continue to strive to convey
To God and you that I'm worthy of a gift that is so
Heavenly.

My undying love for you
Has always propelled me to give you the best of
Me.
I'm so grateful to have you in my life
And to you I leave my
Legacy.

Always Put God First

Sometimes in life
We go through storms
And disasters.
Our lives are not always filled
With good times
And laughter.

Going through these trials
Will build strength
And character.
I know sometimes losing the ones we love
Feels like we are losing
The battle.

The battle is not yours
God will fight it
For you,
Just put God first in your life
And He will see you
Through.

Like the sun after the rain
Bringing sunshine and turning grey skies
Into blue,
God will turn your darkness into light
And shower many blessings down
Upon you.

He will ease your pain
And wipe away all your
Tears.
You are now overwhelmed with the power of his presence
And it feels like your lost loved ones are
Near.

Your faith has allowed you to experience
The word of God
Is True;
He is not only your Father, but He fought every battle
As He carried
You.

Now, you have the strength and character
To continue living a life with purpose here
On earth.
Everything will be alright
As long as you continue to always
Put God First.

God's Creation

Baby girl, never live your life
According to man's
Expectations.
You are above the expectations of man,
Because you are God's
Creation.

God has blessed you with intelligence
And created you in an image of
Great beauty,
With the combination of those magnificent qualities,
You will become everything you ever hoped and dreamed
To be!

Man has tried to take credit for many miracles in which
God has performed in our
Lives.
Love from man will never replace the love of God,
So continue walking your life
With Christ.

Spread your wings
And hold your head up
High,
You will always be a beautiful angel
In our Heavenly Father's
Eyes.

I Feel Your Pain

As your father I feel
Every joy and pain that lives inside
Of you,
Even when I'm the person unknowingly
Causing a roller coaster of emotions by some of the things
I do.

You are truly a gift from God
And I will unconditionally love you
Always.
Never in this lifetime
Will we ever part
Ways.

Even when I go on my journey to meet
Grandpa, Big Momma and Momma Green in
Heaven,
The love I have for you
Will last for infinity times
Seven.

My heart is filled with so much pride
Every time I call your
Name.
You are my daughter and I'm your father
And I pray you will always love me the
Same.

Different Last Names

Tears of pain runs down her face
Like falling
Rain,
Wondering why the man she calls father
Doesn't share her last
Name.

You see, it hurts me so deeply
To see you
Cry,
So I will do my best to explain
To erase those tears from your
Eyes.

When your mother and I first met
You were two months
Old.
I fell in love with you instantly,
Because you were my beautiful
Rose!

You were a gift and a blessing,
I loved you more than
Life!
A few years later your mother and I
Became husband and
Wife!

After years of sharing your pain,
We legally changed your last
Name,
Now our entire family name
Is now one in the
Same.

You see, God up above
Had a greater plan in
Order,
He decided long before you were born
That I would be your
Father!

First Love

The first man a woman
Usually falls in love with is her
Father,
So don't be the first man
To break her
Heart.

You have been given a precious gift
Which is fragile and so
Pure.
When she has a heart that is heavy,
She looks to her father for all the
Cures.

I know if you could,
You would give her the
World;
Just realize giving her support and unconditional love
Is what truly satisfies daddy's little
Girls.

The love you have shown her
From childhood into her adult
Life
Will be the type of love she seeks from her future husband
When she is ready to become a
Wife.

You have now raised a strong and beautiful young woman
And she is a daughter that you are very proud
Of.
Your heart is filled with so much pride
And she will always and forever thank you for being
Her first love.

Born Perfect

I was born with
Divine, beauty, strength and
Intelligence.
I was born with divine gifts
That will forever protect me from the evils of
Men.
I was born with divine sight
To be able to see deeper than the
Surface.
You see, I was born perfect!

You display images
To tell me I'm not pretty
Enough.
You develop irrelevant test
To tell me I'm not smart
Enough.
You even created a plan to try weakening our families,
Thinking that we wouldn't be strong
Enough;
Strong enough to survive
The hatred and disdain you have for our
Skin,
But we have survived it all, because we are divine beings
And all we do is
Win!

Women of Greatness

I'm a child of Almighty God,
He provides me with everything I
Need.
It's time for me to take what's mine
And be all I can
Be!

My journey to greatness
Started high above the clouds in the
Sky
With Bessie Coleman as my pilot,
The first black woman to obtain an aviators license to
Fly.

As I adjust my seat
To make more
Space,
Seated beside me counting money is Madame C. J. Walker,
America's first female self-made millionaire
Of any Race.

Marguerite Annie Johnson was seated next to the window
Writing in her notebook and is one of the most influential
Poets you will ever know.
"I Know Why the Cage Bird Sings,"
Released to wide critical acclaim and you may know her as
Dr. Maya Angelou!

Like my father always said to me,
Education is
Key,
Mary McLeod Bethune, one of the founders of
Bethune - Cookman College was sitting in front of
Me.

She helped to improve educational opportunities for
African Americans near and
Far.
A beautiful statue of her now stands in Washington, DC
At Capitol Hill's
Lincoln Park.

Staying loyal to our dreams
And keeping the faith will take us on a journey to higher
Places.
I look forward to that very special day
When my name is added to this honorary list of
The Women of Greatness!

You Are Never Alone

Many daughters are single mothers
And sometimes it gets hard raising children on your
Own,
I understand, because I'm a man once raised
In a single parent
Home.

It is very sad to say
That some fathers aren't living inside the
Home,
But there is a father who is always with you,
His name is God and with Him, you are never
Alone.

We won't dwell on the negative energy of
Others not doing what they are supposed
To do.
Stay strong and focused on the future of your children,
Because your beautiful kids are depending on
You.

They see you as the provider
And pillar of strength in their
Lives.
From you, your daughter is learning
How to become a woman and your son is learning how to
Treat his future wife.

So, whenever you feel doubt,
Feeling overwhelmed by all the work you
Do
Take a moment to talk to your Father God,
He will give you the wisdom and guidance to help you
Make it through.

Why Do You Fear Us?

We are the aspiring
Young men and women of this
Land,
Educating ourselves
So we won't have to work hard with our
Hands,

But every time we raise
Our hands towards the
Sky,
We see the look of fear
Deep inside your
Eyes.

Don't be afraid,
We won't harm
You.
See, we just want the same opportunities in life
As you
Do.

We will never forget that our people
Were hung from
Trees,
Just for learning
How to write
And read.

Now we understand your fear of us
That's embedded deeply inside of
You.
You are afraid that we may educate ourselves
And take the place of
You.

With great temperament and knowledge
As our weapons of choice for
You
And if you get in our way
We will intellectually destroy
You.
That's why your fear us!

Self - Love

She searched desperately
Trying to fill the void of love in her
Life,
Not realizing the love she had been searching for
Was right before her
Eyes.

Dating different guys for emotional needs
As she looked for
Mr. Right,
But he always turned out to be Mr. Wrong
And would leave her crying through the
Night.

See, men can usually sense when a woman is in a
Desperate need for
Love,
Once you've shown this type of vulnerability
It's you that some men will take
Advantage of.

Love is a very powerful emotion,
It's so amazing what love can
Do,
Especially when the love you are feeling
Comes from God and inside of
You.

Avoid this vicious cycle of
Being hurt by someone
Else.
Spread your pretty wings and fly away
To a peaceful place called
Love of self.

Your Arrival

Racing through the streets
Running red lights
And stop signs,
Making sure I got you and mom
To the hospital in
Time.

This was your day
And I didn't have time to
Waste.
My duty as your father
Was to get you there safely with no
Delays.

I parked the car quickly
In front of the emergency
Doors
And wheeled you and mom
To the triage
Floor.

As I moved the car
Into the proper parking
Space,
One of the nurses greeted me to say,
"Sir, your wife needs you, your baby
Is on the way!"

Now, I'm at mom's bedside
Holding her hand
As we pray,
Praying that you will make it
Into this world
Safely.

Your head is now crowning
And you didn't waste time coming into this
World.
Wow! I'm so excited.
I have been blessed to have you in my life,
My beautiful baby girl!

I will forever thank God for
Giving me the gift of
You.
I will strive to help make
All of your dreams come
True.

My promise to you is to
Introduce you to Christ as we lay both of our hands on the
Bible.
Thank you God for the gift of my beautiful angel
And blessing us with her safe
Arrival.

She Needs You

We are losing our little girls
To a life of vulgarity, sex and immoral
Acts
Broadcasted through radio and television programming,
It's time for us to be fathers and take our daughters
Back.

Have a heart to heart talk with your daughters
And apologize for not being there for her in the
Past.
Listen to her with your heart
As she expresses the pain you have caused her for not being
Her dad.

Take her on father and daughter dates,
Quality time with her is truly
Needed.
You want to be the first man to show your daughter
The proper way a woman should be
Treated.

Your love and acceptance was all she ever wanted.
Now her broken heart has been repaired and feels
Brand-new.
Never walk out of her life again,
Because your beautiful daughter needs
You.

The Ultimate Sacrifice

In so many ways
You've cared for
Me.
You have given the ultimate sacrifice,
Your Son, Jesus Christ who died for
Me.

Father, your love for me is never conditional
It's always the
Same.
That's why I will always worship and pray
To you and only you, in your Son, Jesus
Name.

My Everything

She is the angel that spreads her wings,
Blessing me daily as she makes my heart
Sing,
Songs filled with joy
And for her I will do
Anything.
She is my heart,
My Soul,
My everything.

The tears that sit heavy
Deep inside of my
Eyes,
The miracle that was given to me from
Our Heavenly Father in the
Sky,
The reason why I'm striving
To become a better father and have a strong impact in her
Life,
She is my heart,
My soul,
My everything.

Discipline and Love

I know sometimes
We don't see eye to
Eye.
The love I have for you
Wouldn't allow me to just let things
Slide.

Like a teacher to a student
I'm preparing you for this
World.
You are being raised to become a strong and intelligent
Woman, because this world destroys naive little
Girls.

Discipline never was an easy task
When it came to spanking and talking to
You.
I had to make you aware
That there were consequences in every wrong you
Do.

As we both look back and laugh
About all the differences we've had in
Our lives
My chest is overflowing with
Emotions of love while waterfalls of tears fall down our
Eyes.

I know life hasn't been easy for you
And with love and discipline for the better you have
Changed.
You would make any parent proud of you,
I'm so proud of how far you've
Came.

You will be blessed one day with kids of your very own from
Our Heavenly Father
Above.
They may sometimes go astray,
But will always get back on track
With your discipline and love.

Glitter and Gold

Everything that glitters
Isn't always
Gold.
There is a lot of truth to this saying
And as you continue on this journey called life,
The truth will show.

We should learn to use caution when making decisions
Daily throughout our
Lives,
Because evil is always lurking around the corner to create
Heartache and disaster right before our
Eyes.

Evaluate everyone you meet.
Good intentions are not in the hearts of everyone you
Greet.
Sometimes it's evil in disguise
Ready to turn up the heat while bringing you pain, suffering
And Grief.

God is the answer
To everything that glitters is not
Gold.
All you have to do is open your heart to Him
And He will forever protect your
Soul.

My Swagger

I walk with the inner confidence of
A lion in the
Jungle,
Stepping on any negative energy
Spoken from those who want to see me
Crumble.

My self-esteem is at an all-time high
And yes, I feel like I can touch the
Sky,
Because I have such a strong sense of joy
That I'm feeling deep
Inside!

My joy comes from my Father God;
He gives me everlasting
Love
Giving me the confidence to achieve
Everything I ever
Dreamed of.

The energy I'm feeling
Is a feeling you may never
Understand
Until you allow the love of God to be first in your life
And forever keep His love before the love of
Man.

All for You

He bled and died for you
To make all your dreams come
True.
I would do the same,
Because of my undying love for
You.

You are the reason why
I work so hard to
Provide
A strong foundation of love and support
Unconditionally in your
Life.

Every night I get on my knees
Thanking Jesus for sacrificing His life for
You and me.
Some never had a father here on earth, but we all have a
Father who resides in Heaven and His love stretches further
Than the eyes can see.

I will praise the Lord at all times.
I'm a witness of what His love
Can do.
He has blessed us to experience the unbreakable
Bond between a father and daughter; He did it
All for you.

Education Beyond 4 Walls

Closed in,
Away from the rest of the world for
Hours at a time.
In a room filled with books and teachings
That program our
Minds.

Preparing us for college
So we can live the American
Dream.
Take a look deeper,
Because things are not always what they
Seem.

The American school system teaches us to
Sit still, conform and learn our misguided lessons
To keep things in order.
If we deviate from this organized scheme
Some of us are labeled with ADHD
And other disorders.

If we don't conform
We are stereotyped as having a mind that is abnormal or
Being a troublemaker.
Many of our children are misdiagnosed with ADHD
And are geniuses with superior intelligence blessed from
Our Creator.

We are divine beings
Born with innate gifts to be used as
Blessings.
God created us to be great, create and be of service.
Entrepreneurship is what I will be implementing in my
Lessons.

Our intellect outstretches
Any walls or rules created by
Man.
The education, imagination and aspirations of our children
Will forever be limitless, because their lives are in
God's hands.

The Entrepreneur

I once dreamed a dream of
Running wild and
Free.
No more asking for vacation time,
I just go and come as I
Please.

No more calling in sick
To spend quality time with my
Family,
Because I'm my own boss now
And happily working for me
Is my reality.

Melanin Skin

Black is so powerful and attractive,
So is my pretty black
Skin.
The sun shines so beautiful and bright,
So does my ravishing brown
Skin.
Gold is so precious,
So is my smooth caramel
Skin.
I'm in love with the ravishing power of our precious skin
That is enhanced by the pigment called
Melanin.

Follow Your Dreams

Dreams are ideas
And ideas become
Reality.
Believe in yourself
And you will achieve your goals
Gradually.

Keep God first in your life
And you will do just
Fine,
Because God is good
All the
Time.

Loving You

If he truly loves you
He will fight for you and not against
You.

If he truly loves you
He will encourage you and not discourage
You.

If he truly loves you
He will always be there for you and never give up on
You.

If he truly loves you
He will sacrifice his life to protect
You.

If he truly loves you
He will do whatever it takes to help make your dreams
Come true.

If he truly loves you
Loving you is what he will
Do.

Just Like Me

Loving you is so easy for
Me to
Do,
Especially when I take
One look at
You.

A lot of what you are
Comes from
Me.
Take a look in the mirror
And you will
See.

We both have
The exact same
Smile,
Our eyes will hypnotize anyone
Who looks into them for a
While.

You are very special to me
And I thank God everyday of the
Week
For blessing me with a lovely daughter
Who is just like
Me!

Stay True to You

She worries every day about what others think
And what they would
Say,
Changing the way she walked
And the way she talked every single
Day.

Losing her identity
To blend in with the crowd that she thought was
Cool,
Now she is lost in her web of lies and deception
And doesn't realize who is playing the
Fool.

As she looks into the mirror
A tear falls down her
Eyes.
She washes off the mask of makeup
That is hiding the true strength and beauty she has
Inside.

When going through turbulent times
Life won't get better if you
Run and hide.
Embracing the beautiful person you are while facing your
Battles head on will build great character and a strong sense
Of pride.

She is now empowered by overcoming
The trials she had been going
Through.
You can win every battle, because God is always with you
And I know life isn't easy, but it will become easier if you
Always stay true to you.

Give

Give our women and children
Something to live for,
Not die for.
Give them something
To laugh for,
Not cry for.

Give them a strong sense of pride
To keep their dreams
Alive.
Encourage them with positive affirmations of love
To make them feel good
Inside.

We have too many women and children
With tears in their
Eyes.
C'mon men, we have
To do what's
Right.

Give them the secure
Feeling of comfort
And protection
By wrapping your arms around them
With your love
And affection.

Stay Woke

Yes, systemic racism in America
Will always
Exist,
But through great sacrifice and loss of life,
Leaders of the past have positioned you to achieve
Greatness.

Through these great people
Some of the links in the chains have been
Broken,
But in order to succeed
We must take a stand and walk with our eyes
Open.

Letters to My Daughters

I remember clearly
The first day that I held you in my
Arms,
You would fall fast asleep so peacefully in my chest at night
Knowing I would always protect you from
Harm.

Teaching me how to love unconditionally and naturally
Is what you did for
Me,
Now you've grown to become a beautiful young lady
And I will soon have to set you
Free.

It's going to hurt my heart
To let you
Go,
But I'm sure you will utilize the values
I instilled in you and continue to
Grow.

Diamond, I love you very much
And I wish you the best in this
World.
My first daughter is now going off to college
And I'm so proud of you
Baby girl!

To Breanna,
We are so much alike
From the way we stand to the way we
Smile.
When people see us together they say,
"Yeah, she is your
Child."

You are so appreciative of every moment
We spend together in everything we
Do,
Always ending our father and daughter dates with
Thank you for spending time with me daddy
And I love you.

People always tell me
That you are so
Unique,
From their amazement of your beauty and intellect
Down to the way you dance when you move your
Feet.

Remember to continue to be the individual that
Makes you uniquely
You.
Thank you for always showing me love and appreciation.
You are beautiful and I will
Always love you too!

To Averianna,
You are my honeybun, my baby
And you have been such a blessing in my
Life,
Bringing rays of sunshine and laughter to our family
With the extraordinary talent you possess
Inside.

Always singing and dancing
Putting on one woman
Shows,
We have the best seats in the house
On our couch seated front
Row.

Your youthful energy
Makes me feel so much
Younger,
But I also see great potential in you
To become whatever your mind
Wonders.

A mind with so much creativity
And a heart filled with so much
Love,
I love you and you're my beautiful angel
Sent from Heaven
Above!

I can't end this poem without honoring
A special daughter who has risked her life giving birth
To you three,
She is your mother, my wife and I will love her always.
Together we are one and forever I will feel her heartbeat for
Eternity.

Baby, we are equally yoked,
Meaning, I was made for you and were made for
Me.
We were joined together by our Father God,
And He has blessed us with this beautiful
Family!

Introducing

TRUE COLORS
By
Averianna
Sydnie
Washington

True Colors
by Averianna Sydnie Washington
10 years old.

True colors are here and there
True colors are
Everywhere

We all have our true colors and we should except each other
No matter what color or race, because on the inside we all
Have the same face.

I know you don't think it's fair.
You are always asking, "Why are these colors
Everywhere?"

If you want to know listen clear,
Our lives matter and our true colors will always be
Here.

Stop the killing and hatred towards other colors.
As human beings we should show love and respect towards
One another.

Averianna Sydnie Washington

QUOTES

"I wish that I could always be there for every move you make in this world, because in my heart even as women you will always be daddy's little girls!"

~ Avery Washington

"We all make mistakes, but never allow your mistakes to become your failures."

~ Avery Washington

"Truly loving yourself is to embrace all the imperfections that makes you uniquely beautiful."

~ Avery Washington

"Never will I ever consider myself a minority, because there is nothing minor about my God and me; so when you're speaking of me say majority, because everything is major about my God and me."

~ Avery Washington

"No matter how hard life may get or how rough it seems, continue to take steps forward and follow your dreams."

~ Avery Washington

"Continue spreading your wings and hold your head up high, always remember that you are a woman of greatness in our Heavenly Father's eyes."

~ Avery Washington

"Never live your life according to man's expectations, because you are above the expectations of man; you are God's creation."

~ Avery Washington

"Never sacrifice your love for self for the love of someone else."

~ Avery Washington

"Loving what you are passionate about and being passionate about what you love to do will bring you joy and happiness with success soon following you."

~ Avery Washington

"If you desire an everlasting love that will never fade away,
open up your heart to God, because His love is here to stay."

~ Avery Washington

"Faith combined with self-love will empower you to do great things."

~ Avery Washington

"God has blessed you with an innate gift to be used as a blessing."

~ Avery Washington

"Be mindful that outer beauty is temporary and can easily be erased, but inner beauty is everlasting if your heart is in the right place."

~ Avery Washington

"Your passion is your purpose and your purpose is your ministry!"

~ Avery Washington

"Saying the right words at the right time to the right person can move their life immediately into a positive direction."

~ Avery Washington

"Never become discouraged when others can't see the vision you see, because God has already given divine sight to those He deemed worthy."

~ Avery Washington

"Living in your God given purpose and passion will give you
a joy that's everlasting!"

~ Avery Washington

"Soar beyond your imagination!"

~ Avery Washington

"We must force ourselves to take time daily to enjoy the smells, take deep breaths and enjoy the beautiful blessings of life!"

~ Avery Washington

"Truly knowing your purpose in life will give you the passion and drive to keep your dream alive!"

~ Avery Washington

"Keep doing God's work!"

~ Avery Washington

"Take care of the ones you love and make sure that you are included as one of them."

~ Avery Washington

"Genuinely supporting a loved one's passion will allow you to see the passion from that love one grow for you."

~ Avery Washington

"The willingness to master your God given gift and use it as a blessing to others is a blessing and recipe for greatness!"

~ Avery Washington

"It's a blessing to be a blessing!"

~ Avery Washington

"You've found your divine purpose the moment you find yourself extremely passionate about performing a service."

~ Avery Washington

"Never seek the approval of man for the gifts God has bestowed upon you with His very own hands."

~ Avery Washington

"Make sure that you always have an undying love for you."

~ Avery Washington

"Your purpose is your blessing!"

~ Avery Washington

About The Author

Avery Washington was born and raised in New Orleans, Louisiana and is one of the most respected authors and poet in the world today. He is a very passionate writer who has combined his great gift of storytelling and poetry into powerful collections of heartfelt writings in which we all can relate to daily. Mr. Washington allows the reader to experience every emotion as he intellectually stimulates minds with rhythm and rhyme as he tells stories of empowerment, inspiration, love and awareness.

To learn more about Avery Washington, visit his author site at: www.averywashington.com

Acknowledgments

Angela W. Patton
Founder of Camp Diva / CEO of Girls For A Change
Girls For A Change
2710 Swineford Road
North Chesterfield, VA 23237
www.girlsforachange.org

Mailing Address   Phone: 866-738-4422

California   Virginia
P.O. Box 1436   P.O. Box 14844
San Jose, CA 95109   Richmond, VA 23221

Shirley A Crews Taylor, MA
President/Principal Consultant
TCT Enterprises, LLC (TCTE)
P.O. Box 720464, Houston, TX 772721
www.tctenterprisesllc.com
info@tctenterprisesllc.com
Phone: 281-383-9523
Fax: 281-962-4963

Beautifully Said Magazine
'Twins of Media'
La Trisha McIntosh and La Tasha Taylor
Founder/Editor-in-Chief
info@beautifullysmagazine.com
http://beautifullysmagazine.com
832-755-5034

Be Admired Designs
Kisha Washington
beadmireddesigns@gmail.com
281-972-5570

Divine Angels Learning Academy
Freddie & Shon Williams (Owners)
12331 Murphy Rd.
Stafford, TX 77477
281-495-3700

Land & Destination Experts
Cruise Planners
Debra McGregor
www.affordableluxurytravel.net
#destinationsbydebra
832-447-1323

Thank you for supporting *LEGACY*!

www.ingramcontent.com/pod-product-compliance
Lightning Source LLC
Chambersburg PA
CBHW071232090426
42736CB00014B/3048